The Rubais
of
Rumi

The Rubais of Rumi

Insane with Love

Translations and commentary by
NEVIT O. ERGIN and WILL JOHNSON

Inner Traditions
Rochester, Vermont

Inner Traditions
One Park Street
Rochester, Vermont 05767
www.InnerTraditions.com

Library of Congress Cataloging-in-Publication Data
Jalal al-Din Rumi, Maulana, 1207–1273.
  [Ruba'iyat. English]
  The rubais of Rumi : insane with love / translations and commentary by Nevit O.
Ergin and Will Johnson.
     p. cm.
  Summary: "The first English translation of the rubais of Rumi"—Provided by
publisher.
  ISBN-13: 978-1-59477-183-5
  ISBN-10: 1-59477-183-9
  I. Ergin, Nevit Oguz, 1928– II. Johnson, Will, 1946– III. Title.
  PK6481.R8E5 2007
  891'.5511—dc22

                                                              2007021369
Printed and bound in the United States by Lake Book Manufacturing

10 9 8 7 6 5 4 3 2 1

Text design and layout by Priscilla Baker
This book was typeset in Sabon, with Centaur used as a display typeface

To send correspondence to the authors of this book, mail a first-class letter to the
authors c/o Inner Traditions • Bear & Company, One Park Street, Rochester, VT 05767,
and we will forward the communication.

Contents

*I*ntroduction

Rubais are the twelve-bar blues of Persian poetry: a literary form whose meters, rhyming patterns, and rhythms resonated as deeply and naturally in the souls of the early poets of Persia as did the chord changes and rhyming patterns of the songs that Robert Johnson and Blind Lemon Jefferson would play for the patrons of the roadhouses in the southern United States in the early part of the twentieth century. The most well-known collection of rubais, dating from the eleventh century, is still *The Rubaiyat of Omar Khayyam,* a story in verse about life lived to its fullest written by a true Renaissance man (Khayyam was a mathematician, philosopher, scientist, and astronomer as well as a gifted poet) several centuries before the Renaissance in Italy would give the Western world this term.

It was only natural, then, that a century after Khayyam, the great Islamic poet, mystic, and creator of the dance of the whirling dervish, Jallalludin Rumi, would craft rubais of his own and add his own particular flavor of sparkle to the tradition. Unlike Khayyam, who

1

carefully crafted his poems in private and put pen to paper, Rumi was more of an ecstatic street rapper, a spontaneous wordsmith who would speak and compose his poems on the spot as he wandered around his adopted town of Konya, stopping now and then to talk to anyone who would listen. Fortunately for us, his closest followers would walk with him and record the words that poured like a torrent from their beloved teacher's mouth.

Rubais can also be considered a Persian form of Japanese haiku: short and pithy aphorisms and observations about life, whose depth and message often belie the brevity of their form. Like the best songs of our modern era, a great deal can be conveyed in just a few, short phrases, and some even read like a tantalizing poetic pitch for a feature-length film script. Their precision and directness well suited Rumi's wish to convey profound spiritual truths and instructions in a simple form that the townspeople of Konya could understand and resonate with. Even so, very few of Rumi's rubais have yet been translated into the languages of the contemporary Western world.

The explanation for Rumi's continued popularity is that he expresses the most profound and complex truths in the most simple and beautiful language. These truths are balm for the heart and soul. They show us a remedy for healing the painful barbs of yearning, longing, and disappointment that stab at us so incessantly. They suggest a way to reconnect ourselves with what we feel we've been separated from. They tell us to go back to ourselves. There, and only there, can we find what we're looking for.

This is the mystic's secret, and Rumi reveals it to us. The mystical quest, far from being the exclusive plaything of a few unusually gifted, and perhaps a bit strange, individuals, is the birthright of us all. We're all on this quest, Rumi tells us, and anything less than a complete dissolving into what he calls the world of union isn't ultimately going to satisfy us.

So where do you go to begin this quest? Rumi is very clear that you need to go into yourself and examine who and what you are and what it is you find there. Paradoxically, it is only through going into yourself that you can get beyond yourself. Through the profound transformation that took place in him through the companionship and spiritual play with his great friend Shams, he came to understand that orthodox religion—with its books, laws, rules, and rituals—was unwittingly keeping its adherents from experiencing this transformation for themselves. The mystical embrace is available to all of us, but the only way to enter into it is through a direct, personal experience. Faith and belief in anything that cannot be directly experienced, no matter how attractive and alluring it may be to the mind, just isn't going to be able to deliver on its promise.

The rubais in this volume are among our favorites from the more than 1,700 rubais that Rumi spontaneously composed. Some of them delight with their simple imagery; others quietly reveal the most profound spiritual truths and visions. Many of them are funny (a few of them are just plain quirky). Some of them will leave you feeling uplifted. With others, it may feel like being cut with a knife.

As wonderful a poet as Rumi is, he is also a profound spiritual teacher. Seeded in the rubais' few lines are little spiritual hints that can become the basis for serious spiritual practices. To guide you in understanding the experiences that Rumi is speaking of, I have created the following chapter that provides short explanations of the themes found throughout Rumi's work: separation and union; existence and absence; annihilation (or melting down); ecstasy and intoxication; the friend; the beloved; the lover; the cupbearer; and sema. It is our hope that this brief exploration of themes will help you to go beyond the words into the direct experience that Rumi so constantly tells us is our birthright.

I honestly don't think it's possible for anyone not to identify personally with at least some of the poems in the pages to come, feeling even that Rumi is speaking, across time and space, directly to you. Indeed, you are exactly whom he is speaking to, and each rubai can be considered a personal invitation for you to come out and play in the fields of ecstasy. So read these little nuggets as inspiration and advice from a close friend from across the ages who cares about your heart and soul and knows how to help you. Chew them slowly, and see if you can extract all their taste and meaning. What are they saying? What are they suggesting? What are they encouraging you to do? Can you accept the invitation?

WILL JOHNSON
MAPLE BAY, BRITISH COLUMBIA
SEPTEMBER 2006

The Themes of Rumi's World

Separation and Union

During the nine months of gestation, as it grows and develops inside the womb, a child is at one with its mother. All of its emotional needs are satisfied, its physical requirements met, by the watery environment in which it floats. At the moment of its birth, however, as it parts from its mother, it enters into the rough and tumble world of separation, and so begins the long and often arduous journey of individuating oneself and becoming a fully independent, fully functional human being that can live and stand on its own.

To grow into such an independent entity, separate and distinct from everything else it can perceive to exist outside of its physical body, is the newborn soul's first task, and people who are not able to successfully complete this task and individuate themselves in this way often have great difficulty in the world.

The consciousness that passes as normal in the world at large, collectively developed by millions of humans over untold thousands of years, is a consciousness of separation. While every one of us may find that we possess unique and different talents that make us unique and different people, we nonetheless share the exact same identity and sense of self with everyone else: We experience ourselves as an entity named "I" (we all have the same name for ourselves) that is somehow poured, like milk into a container, into our physical bodies, and everything that exists inside our body is exclusively "me" while everything that exists outside our body is "other than me." This is the experiential formula on which the mathematics of separation is founded.

What could be more normal than to identify yourself with the voice inside your head that calls itself "I?" We all do this. We all have to do this. The problem, however, is that the consciousness of separation comes with a shadow side as well, and this shadow side causes us a great deal of suffering. Along with the feelings of genuine accomplishment that accompany independence and successful individuation comes a lurking sense of anxiety, fear, disconnection, and painful alienation. Separation hurts and is scary. We stand alone and look out onto a world of which we're not a part. Where do we fit into this larger world that we feel so separate from? Where did the soil that we now feel so uprooted from go to? Is there not some way to get back to the garden—or reach forward to a new one?

Rumi provides us with answers. The individuated soul, if it still wants the contentment that it inherently knows to be its birthright, must undertake its second task. It needs to let go of the consciousness of separation that it has worked so hard and successfully to establish and birth itself into a new world in which it feels naturally merged and unified with everything that is. We started our life in the embrace of our mother's womb. We were expelled into the world of separation. Now it's time to enter forward into the larger embrace of what Rumi calls union.

The consciousness of union is every bit as real and palpable as the consciousness of separation, whose pains can only be healed when we once again feel this natural and intimate connection with the larger world of the earth and the heavens and everything that exists. Rumi tells us that if we want to reclaim our birthright we have to go beyond ourselves. If we dig our heels in instead and hold on tightly to our sense of separate self, then we'll stay stuck in the hurts and upsets of the conventional world of separation.

Rumi exhorts us to surrender to the tugs and pulls of union, to let its currents sweep us away and take us wherever they want. If we can yield in this way to these currents (and these currents are active in each and every one of us), if we can submit to the forces we feel stirring inside us and listen to their voices (they speak clearly and eloquently in the wordless language of feelings and sensation), then we can undertake the journey that leads to union.

Union is a feeling state in which inner and outer come back together as one. Union is always beckoning us back into its embrace. The impulse to union is as natural a feeling in human beings as is our impulse to love and to take a mate, and it is this impulse that launched the great monotheistic religions of Islam and Judaism.

The monotheistic revolution was based on a dawning awareness of a place of experience that felt one with the world. Truly one. One as a lived, felt experience; not one as a belief or an aspiration. The seminal figures in these religious movements must have been so moved and overwhelmed by their direct experience of oneness and union that they naturally felt an intense urgency to share it with everyone in their tribe. Worship multiple idols, they might say, and your mind and heart get muddied and troubled. But as soon as you feel and realize that everything (and if the concept of God isn't intended to include and mean "everything," then what could it possibly be referring to?) can come together as one—no you and everything else—then your mind and heart and body become imbued with a feeling awareness that aligns you with what can only be the energies of God. In the words of the *shema*, the most sacred phrase of Judaism: listen, children of God, the world is of one piece.

Union is everyone's birthright, and it doesn't matter if you're a Muslim, a Jew, a Buddhist, a Christian, a nature worshipper, an atheist, an agnostic, or absolutely whatever: it's yours for the taking and the asking. You earned this birthright just by being born, but you do have to go and claim it.

Rumi tells us to go to union. It's where we leave our suffering behind. He tells all of us to do it on an individual basis, and he serves as a cry and invitation for all people of all faiths to do it on a collective basis as well. Rumi was revered not only by the Muslim community of Konya in which he lived and taught; he was also loved by the Jews and Christians of Konya as well. When asked about this, the Jews would say that, when Rumi spoke, they understood the teachings of Moses; the Christians would say that, through his words, the words of Jesus came alive to them.

When the spirit of scriptural texts is overlooked in favor of a literal reading of the words, divisions and rivalries among religions naturally ensue, most often with tragic results. Rumi encourages all of us to go beyond the confines and limitations of the orthodox face of religion and to reach back to the original experience on which all the religions were founded. He urges us to fall back into the center of ourselves, back into that common ground of being that we share identically with each and every person who has ever lived, that place in which we are no longer Muslim, no longer Jewish, no longer Christian, but simply human. It is perhaps for this reason that UNESCO (the United Nations Educational, Scientific, and Cultural Organization), whose mission is to encourage peace and universal respect by promoting collaboration among nations and peoples, has declared 2007 to be The Year of Rumi in honor of his birth eight hundred years ago. Separation in oneself, or among cultures, nations, and religions, is no longer a viable position to hold and embody. Only the lived experience of union can put to rest our individual suffering and help heal the tragic conflicts of religion.

Existence and Absence

Do you remember daydreaming as a child? Perhaps you were lying on your back in a summer field looking up at the clouds passing across the sky. Or maybe you found that staring out of the schoolroom window, and letting your mind drift, was more interesting than the lesson being taught in class. In both instances, even though your body was physically present, your mind was somewhere else. What Rumi calls *absence* is akin to a kind of divine daydream, one that takes you out of yourself and transports you to God.

We are all born into existence and learn to live by the rules of this world. We learn how to focus our attention and be present to whatever is occurring. At other times, however, we may feel the tugs of union pulling at us in another direction entirely, one in which our attention begins to waver and we no longer see the objects of our world so clearly even though our eyes are still wide open. In these

moments, the energies of what Rumi calls God start drawing us out
of ourselves. We become absent to ourselves, but present to God.

The experience of absence and the consciousness of union are
closely aligned. When we enter into union, we leave the world of sep-
aration behind, and our awareness of being a specific person (named
I) living in this present moment may begin to fade away. We may
even enter into a kind of trance in which we become momentarily
lost to ourselves. But in our place we find God. When the egoic fic-
tion of the mind begins to loosen its tight grip on our consciousness,
we can easily slip into absence instead.

My partner once told me at length about the absences she would
enter into as a child. It would start out as a kind of daydream. Then
she would lose her conventional awareness of self and enter into a
warm world in which her body felt like it was glowing and the world
she looked out onto would burst into golden light. Once she was out
in a rowboat with her older sister when one of her absences seized
her. The world became saturated with the most beautiful light imag-
inable. In this state she rose to her feet, her arms outstretched, and
called out to her sister:

"Lynda, Lynda, can't you see it?! It's sooooooo beautiful!"

To which her sister replied: "Sit down! You're rocking the
boat!"

Absence rocks the boat of existence. If we're lodged firmly in the
consciousness of separation, we may feel concerned for our friends
and family members who succumb to absence's pull. We worry for
their well-being and their safety, but we needn't. While it may look
strange to an observer, absence feels welcomed by those fortunate
enough to have been seized by it. As the trance dancers of the rave
movement can attest, surrendering to absence, while it may look

unconventional (and we live in a world in which it is conventional not to move the body very much at all), brings with it an ecstasy that makes giving up the conventional easy to do.

Annihilation (or Melting Down)

There is a famous Sufi saying that, in order to reach God in this life, we need to die before we die. This in no way implies the premature death of the body. What needs to die, what needs to be melted down like jewelry that is heated to a high temperature so it can be recast in a new and different shape, is our belief in ourselves as separate, insular beings disconnected from one another as well as from the larger world in which we live. Rumi tells us that, by exposing and knocking down the props that support that belief (the many tensions that we carry in our bodies and our minds, the many concepts we may hold about reality that we have accepted on faith but never, perhaps, critically examined), we, in effect, experience the death of that belief while still alive, and the doors to heaven on earth open before us.

Fana is ordinarily translated into English as "annihilation," but this is perhaps too harsh a word and may be misleading as well. In fana, we don't aggressively pulverize or crush the mind of separation; we melt it down instead. The self needs to be understood and befriended first. Then it naturally can melt down and dissolve its rigidities.

The path to fana starts exactly where you are and goes right into and through the self. If we develop any hatred toward the self and interpret annihilating it as destroying it, we only succeed in further frustrating ourselves by demolishing the way that leads to fana. Better that we melt it down instead and recast it in a different form. In poem after poem Rumi keeps pleading for help in breaking free from the spell cast by the egoic self for, when that entire quality of the mind can be melted down and put to rest, our troubles and suffering also melt away. Dying to ourselves in this moment, we are reborn here and now in the embrace of the consciousness of union.

The Sufis tell us that there are two worlds: this world and the other world. In Christianity, in contrast, the two worlds that are spoken of are this world and the next world, the world we pass over to when we die. The devout Christian believes that, if he leads a good Christian life, he will die and go to heaven. The Sufi, however, is not willing to wait that long. Why not go to heaven here and now, before the physical body tires and dies? For the Sufi, fana is a direct experience of the divine while still very much alive in this body. In fana we travel beyond ourselves, far, far away to a different realm without necessarily having to move a muscle or take a single step. Zen Buddhism has acknowledged the person who has entered fana in this way:

> gone, gone
> gone beyond
> gone altogether beyond
> what ecstasy!
> hallelujah!

Ecstasy and Intoxication

Ordinarily we think of spiritual practice, with its images of monks and nuns praying in cells or meditating silently in zendos for long hours, days, and weeks at a time, as sober and serious undertakings.

Rumi's spirituality, however, is anything but a sober affair. Rumi loves the ecstatic dancer (and became one himself) who loses herself in surrendering to the movements of her body, and he avoids the sober theologian who tries to convince us with his arguments (that come across as a touch sterile). For Rumi, reason when applied to religion is an impediment to God; the real action of religion is an ecstatic explosion of energies through the body and mind that may leave us looking like a happy drunk on a bender.

There is some controversy as to exactly what kind of wine Rumi keeps urging us to get drunk on. Certainly he is referring to the divine wine of bodily sensation itself that, once kindled and activated, releases forth powerful and profound energies that we have no choice but to surrender to and become totally intoxicated by. Once these bodily energies awaken and start moving in and through us, we may look very drunk indeed.

However, most of us most of the time have little awareness of the divine wine that is bottled up in our body. Research studies suggest that we are using only 5 to 15 percent of the capability and capacity of our brains, but what is also true is that we probably only feel, at any given moment, between 5 and 15 percent of the full range of tactile sensations that fill our body from head to foot. Sensation (wild, alive, vibrant, ecstatic) can be felt to exist on every part of the body down to the smallest cell, but many (more reasonable) people never take advantage of the invitation to drink from this divine open bar.

Rumi exhorts us to rekindle an awareness of body as a field of ecstatic, vibratory sensation. As a young man he was taught by his father, who himself was an accomplished mystic, the doctrine of *ma'iyya*, which tells us that God cannot be found in the mind alone, and not even in the heart but needs to be felt as a physical sensation in each and every part of the body.

Islam strictly forbids the consumption of alcohol. Even so, Rumi's shattering revelation during his retreats with his great friend Shams showed him a path beyond the rules and regulations of organized religion. It is known, for example, that Shams would tell Rumi to purchase and consume wine as a way to push his friend beyond his attachment to the orthodox ways.

Music and dance are also prohibited in the strictest vision of Islam, and we know that Rumi went far beyond that prohibition. He would keep urging the musicians to keep playing longer so he could keep moving his body in response to the impulses he felt deep within. The word *ecstasy* can be thought of as *ex-stasis*, or the coming out of a condition of stillness, and who is less still than the wild dancer surrendering to whatever movements want to erupt through his body?

In any case, Rumi tells us that the cautious and sober-minded person is never going to fall into God's embrace. Become drunk on the divine, and then drink some more. Rumi wants us to turn ourselves into raging, divine alcoholics, wildly drunk on the energies of God, and certainly this vision is a breath of fresh air for all of us who have felt the longing in our hearts to reunite with the energies of the divine, but who never have been able to satisfy that longing through the sober rituals and ceremonies that take place in the more orthodox churches, mosques, temples, meditation halls, and ashrams of this world.

The Friend, the Beloved, the Lover, the Cupbearer

Rumi populates his poems with a cast of recurring characters that includes the friend, the beloved, the lover, and the cupbearer. Because so much of his spiritual opening occurred through his friendship and relationship with Shams, it is often difficult to know whether he is talking about an actual person or a divine counterpart when he invites these people into his poetry. Indeed, in many ways those distinctions became blurred to Rumi as well as he certainly looked upon Shams as a direct conduit to God.

The friend is our partner in the practice, the person with whom we sit down and gaze, with whom we get up and dance, with whom we share our deepest longings, our joys, and our pains. In the presence of the friend, we dissolve back into union. Rumi and Shams took the concept of friendship to an entirely new level: two individuals coming together not just to enjoy each other's companionship, but to merge with each other through dissolving the boundaries that ordinarily keep us so isolated and separate. In this deeply merged place, the two individual presences are replaced by the unitary presence of the divine. Fortunate are those of us who can meet a friend like this as a real, flesh and blood person.

In the language of Sufism, however, the friend also refers to that indwelling spirit that always patiently awaits an invitation to come out and play, that special place in our body and mind in which we feel the presence of God coming closer. We all have this same friend inside ourselves, but we actively have to pursue this friendship. Rumi tells us to quit running away from ourselves. He urges us to turn around, go inside, and befriend ourselves instead. What we discover at our deepest core becomes our special friend, whether we have an actual partner in the practice or not.

The beloved is what we long for more than anything else. In separation we feel cut off and disconnected from the greater universe in which we live. Deep inside our hearts we yearn to feel connected to everything that is, and there's no more powerful desire to be found in any heart. Rumi tells us that the only way to satisfy that yearning is to encounter the beloved, to embrace the beloved, to be swept away by the beloved.

Many translators prefer to equate the beloved with God, but that may sound somehow too large or grand a notion. The beloved may be as large as the universe, but as Rumi tells us, it can fit inside a space in the heart that is as small as the eye of a needle. The beloved is what happens to you when you're melted away and floating along in union's current. As Rumi says, everything comes and goes; only the beloved is irreplaceable in this world. Without awareness of the beloved, we wander around in separation's spell.

The path of the Sufi always proceeds through the felt energies of the heart. Rumi encourages all of us to become lovers for it is through an opening to love that most of us feel our hearts stirred. Two people fall in love (be it a platonic love or a love of sexual mating) because of the palpable attraction that they feel between them, but what they're more likely falling in love with is the presence of the beloved that they feel when they're with their lover. Once that bond of love has been established between two people, then the real work begins, and Rumi is very clear that love is not just pleasure and joy. The spark that is created at the meeting of lovers stirs the pot of the soul and significantly turns up the heat underneath it. Impurities come rushing to the surface, and all hell can break loose. But Rumi keeps telling us that troubles are a part of love, that troubles are one of love's ways of healing us. Run away from the troubles, and you run away from the love. Love can be rough as well as gentle, but fall in love all the same. If the thought of love's rough troubles scares you off, then it is unlikely that you'll ever fall in love. But if you don't know love, how can you meet the beloved?

The friend, the beloved, and the lover are often interchangeable terms, and, on a human level, how could you not fall in love with a friend who came into your life and sparked something in you that took you both to God? In that Rumi viewed the person of Shams as the actual link through which he was able to reconnect himself back to the energies of God, the boundaries between real people and their divine counterparts are blurry ones indeed. As you read the poems, you may find it illuminating to read them both ways, first as referring to a real person and an actual event, second as speaking directly about the symbolic friend and beloved.

The cupbearer is a kind of divine wine steward. Rumi tells us that, when the currents of union begin to get stirred, help and guidance from unseen sources start showing up in our lives. What could be of more help in this passionate play of becoming drunk on the divine than to have your very own personal wine steward standing at your table filling your glass the moment it becomes empty? Rumi begs the cupbearer to keep on filling his glass, over and over again, and never to let it go dry.

Is Shams the friend? Is Shams the beloved? Is Shams the cupbearer? Or are these personages something else altogether?

You decide.

Sema

Rumi tells us that we can't just wish the energies of God to come alive in us. We need to do intentional practices that directly affect the physiology in the body and the thought patterns in the mind. And we need to do these practices day after day after day.

The practice that *sema* most traditionally refers to is the dance of the whirling dervish (a dervish is a Sufi mystic). Many of us have seen images of whirling dervishes from Rumi's Mevlevi order in Turkey dressed in white, flowing robes with tall, black felt hats turning around in circles to the sound of the drum and the ney. The Mevlevi Sufi would say that everything in the world, from the smallest atom to our largest planets, spins on its own axis. This constant motion of revolution is so fundamental to the workings of the universe that only through consciously participating in this motion can we align ourselves with the energies of God. Through the rituals and practices of whirling, the dervish can temporarily leave this world behind and spin off into a different world, one in which the currents of union and the energies of fana are felt strongly.

There is some controversy as to how and where the practice of whirling came into Rumi's life. Some chroniclers have suggested that Shams taught the practice to Rumi during their retreats together. Another chronicler suggests that it originated one day out of the overwhelming grief that Rumi felt at the departure and loss of Shams. According to this account, Rumi was in an outdoor garden one afternoon, beside himself with pain and grief. In the garden were several tall pillars that were connected to each other by an overhead trellis on which grapes or figs would grow. Rumi is said to have leaned against one of the pillars, crying and shaking. Holding on to the pil-

Boca Raton Downtown Library

Items that you checked out

Title: The rubais of Rumi : insane with love /
translations and commentary by Nevit O.
Ergin and Will Johns

ID: 3365604286089

Due: Thursday, October 28, 2021

Renewed to
Nov 15

Total items: 1
Account balance. $0.00
9/28/2021 1 42 PM
Checked out: 2
Overdue: 0
Hold requests: 0
Ready for pickup: 0

Thank you for using the bibliotheca SelfCheck
System.

lar with one hand, he began turning himself around it, round and round, faster and faster, not being able to stop until the grief and pain he was feeling had literally been spun out of him.

In addition to the act of turning, Rumi repeatedly mentions three other practices in his poems and urges his followers to explore them. By far the most often cited practice in all of Rumi's poetry is the practice of sitting with your beloved friend, holding each other's gaze, not looking away, relaxing completely into the feeling generated through the contact of your shared gaze, and surrendering to the powerful shifts in physical sensation and consciousness that naturally occur. His poems give compelling evidence that this was the primary practice that he and Shams fell into and explored behind the closed doors of their retreat room. Over time, the apparent solidity of the body and mind begin to dissolve, and the partners in the practice merge their consciousness into a shared perception of union. The practice is both extremely simple and very powerful.

Many of Rumi's poems speak of the spiritual benefits that come from abstaining from food. It is known that he and Shams would often forego eating for long periods of time while they were sequestered in their retreat room. Anyone who has had any experience at all with fasting knows that the changes that occur over the days are not just felt at the level of the body. Emotions get stirred and resolved. The mind often becomes much clearer. Underneath the blanketing layer of thought, union is to be found, and Rumi understood that fasting could powerfully assist us in opening to union.

Finally, in many of the longer poems not included in this volume, Rumi talks about how different patterns of breath can either enslave us in the world of separation or liberate us into the world of union. Our breath is a direct reflection of the relative ease or agony that we feel in our body and mind in the present moment. Are there any kinks or tensions in our body that stop our breath from moving fully and freely? By learning to soften and release the kinks and tensions, our breath automatically becomes easier and fuller. We become more closely and naturally aligned with the life force itself.

Movement, gazing, fasting, breathing: just as union is everyone's birthright, so do the very same practices work for people of all faiths and backgrounds. To the question "how do I get to union?" the answer is the same as the punch line to the joke about how to get to Carnegie Hall: practice.

The Rubais

hear this if you can:

if you want to reach him

you have to go beyond yourself

and when you finally arrive at the land of absence

be silent

don't say a thing

ecstasy, not words, is the language spoken there

there is a plain beyond Islam and infidelity both
our love rests in the middle of that plain
that's where the sage goes to bow down
because there's no room there for either the
believer or the infidel

❧

you are a volume in the divine book
a mirror to the power that created the universe
whatever you want, ask it of yourself
whatever you're looking for can only be found
inside of you

don't waste time pining for the past

don't hold regrets for things that happened long ago

if you let the past go, you'll be a Sufi

you'll be the child of the present moment

the young and old of now

o my God

don't leave me to the hand of this slippery self

don't let me kneel down before anyone but you

I run to you from all the tricks and troubles

of "myself"

I'm yours

don't send me back to myself

whoever sees you with the eyes of the heart

goes ecstatic

but the blind person stays lost in thought

hundreds of branches from the secret worlds are

dropping roses at your feet

why do you cut down the tree of contentment?

a different kind of fragrance

comes from the gathering of lovers

a different kind of drunkenness

comes from those wise in love

the knowledge you learned in school is different

love is something else altogether

I was a pious man

but you made me sing songs

you had me disrupt the gathering

and sent me to find wine

I was sitting on a prayer rug like a dignified elder

but you turned me into a joke for street kids

A person who's sober

is like a horse that's worth less than its saddle

it doesn't matter if you're all dressed up in gold

if you haven't been to the tavern

you can't yet be considered a man

because the smell of wine

is at the bottom

of every true religion

don't be a scholar

be a fool for love instead

if you're the moon in the sky, fall down

become dirt on the road

be together with young and old, good and bad

if you start out as a pawn

you'll become the king later on

reason, get lost

there's no room for you here

even if you turned yourself into a single hair

you still couldn't fit inside love

morning comes, but that doesn't change a thing

whatever candle you lit in your mind

would look foolish in front of the sun

your love has left me exhausted and worn out

I can't eat during the day

or sleep at night

really, your love has turned me into my own

worst enemy

they appraised my head, my turban, and my robe

but they wouldn't even give me a dime

haven't you heard my name in the world?

I am Nothing

I am Nothing

know this very well:

lovers can never be devout Muslims

in the religion of love there's no room for faith

no room for heresy

no self, no reason

not even heart or soul

whoever's not like that isn't a lover

good or bad

visible or hidden

everything is under God's command

I strive so hard

but fate keeps telling me:

"there are so many things beyond your control"

❧

you can't untie this knot by listening to

fairy tales

you have to do something inside yourself

the smallest fountain inside of you

is better than a raging river outside

if you let God hunt you

you'll be free of all your sorrows

but if you chase after your desires

you'll stay a slave to yourself

know this very well:

your sense of self is an obstacle on your way

you'll keep getting beat up

if you just hang around with yourself

o my choice beauty

you've gone

but your love remains in my heart

your image in my eye

o guide on my winding road

I keep turning round and round in the hopes of

finding you

not until the mosques and minarets come

tumbling down

will real peace enter into our lives

not before faith becomes heresy

and heresy becomes faith

will any man of God become truly Muslim*

---

*What an incendiary statement! But it is important to understand that Rumi is
not finding fault with Islam per se. His criticism is directed toward the tendency
on the part of all religions to enshrine orthodox beliefs that unwittingly prevent
their followers from having a direct experience of the insight on which the reli-
gions were founded. Instead of speaking of mosques and Muslims, Rumi could
just as easily be referring to churches and Christians or synagogues and Jews.

the secrets of the mind's attainment

can only be found in madness

whoever has become insane with love

becomes the wisest one of us all

whoever gets familiar with the mysteries of

the heart

becomes a complete stranger to himself

I was just a particle

but you made me bigger than a mountain

I was lagging behind

but you put me in front

you repaired my broken heart

and left me hand-clapping drunk

if even a tiny piece of yourself remains

in existence

you're still worshipping idols

but if you break free of all doubt and suspicion

only with the ax of reason

then you create a new false idol

called self-confidence

soul flies out of the body at the time of death

and throws the body away like an old piece

of clothing

it gives the body that was made of dust

back to the dust of the earth

and merges with its old radiance

if you could be the real master of yourself

for even a single moment

the knowledge of all the prophets would be

revealed to you

that beauty of absence

the one the whole world is chasing after

would appear as a perfect reflection

on the mirror of your mind

I made an oath to myself:

as long as I live

as long as my soul remains in this body

I won't deviate from the right way

but later I looked to my left and then to

my right

and I saw our beloved everywhere

how could I make a wrong turn?

I'm faith and heresy both

I'm clear and muddy

old and wizened

yet as young as a newborn babe

when I die, don't say that I'm dead

say, "he was dead and came back to life

the beloved took him away"

if you're nimble on God's path
you'll rise up to the sky
your real place is on that throne
aren't you ashamed of just being a shadow
dragging along on the ground?

❦

love entered me
and became blood in my veins
emptied me of myself
and filled me with the beloved
every single particle of my body
is soaked in the beloved
my name is all that's left of me
he became the rest

there is a place beyond good and bad deeds both

but this is not the place for every young and

pretty novice

the price for the one who wants to get there

is to give his life

and sacrifice his heart

the one who cuts your neck

is the one who suffers your sorrow

the one who crowns you

is the one who tricks you and covers up

your modesty

the one who loads you with good

is the one who burdens you

your real friend

is the one who takes you away from yourself

it is love's custom to drink from the fountain
of faith
love doesn't worry about life or bread
love's table is set beyond day or night
then what is fasting?
fasting is an invitation to the secret feast

fasting purifies you and lets you rise up to the sky
you'll get burned up like a candle
illuminated by fasting's fire
but if you become the slave of food
the darkness from that morsel will turn you into
a morsel for the ground

o moonfaced

if you are in love with our love

then get out of the petrified layers of this world

come to the sea of heart

why do you stay at the edge of a creek?

❧

the slave of love was with the moon of

soul yesterday

and asked a difficult question

the answer never came

but the one who asked the question disappeared

time cuts short this uproar

death's wolf tears this flock to pieces

everyone carries some pride in his head

but the slap of death comes sooner or later

when this life ends

God gives us a different life

when our temporary life is finished

God shows us another one

love is the water of life

so jump right in

there's new life in every drop of that sea

if your hands get tired serving the beloved

then use your feet

if your feet get tired

then yell and scream

if you lose your voice

then use your head

in other words, show your faith in every breath

you take

it's so nice to move from one place to another

to flow like running water

and not to freeze in any one spot

yesterday and all its words have gone

we have to find new words today

I'm in love with love

and love is in love with me

body is in love with soul

and soul is in love with body

sometimes I encircle love's neck with my arms

sometimes love

like a heart stopping beauty

throws his arms around me

there's a Soul deep inside your soul

search for that Soul

there's a jewel in the mountain of your flesh

go and find the mine of that jewel

o wandering Sufi, search if you can

but not somewhere outside

look for it inside yourself

why are you running around the village of your fancy

why are you washing your eyes with blood from

your heart

God is in your being from your head to your toenail

o one who doesn't know who you are

what are you looking for beside yourself?

when love picks someone

troubles start raining down on his head

Mansur* revealed a hint of love's secret

and was hung from the rope of jealousy

---

*Mansur was a Sufi saint who was put to death by the orthodox authorities for having had the audacity to say what is true for all of us: that we are all the source of truth.

come again, come again

whoever you are, come again

even if you're an infidel

if you worship fire or idols

come again

ours is not a pathway of despair

even if you've broken your promise a hundred

times over

still, come again

childhood has passed

youth has flown away

old age comes around

every guest is treated nicely for only three days

get up my friend

and ride your donkey faster

when we were children
we listened to our teacher
later we continued our learning
by gazing at our friend's face
see what happened when we stopped talking?
we came as a cloud
but we left like the wind

beloved said to me:

"since you buy kisses from every beauty

why don't you buy one from me?"

"with gold?" I asked

"no," he said

"what can I do with gold?"

"with life?" I asked again

"yes, yes," said he

how amazing that the beloved fits in my heart

that the souls of a thousand bodies fit inside

this body

there are thousands of harvests in a single grain

and hundreds of universes pass through the eye

of a needle

while sailing on a boat

a man looks at the shore

and thinks that the reed beds are moving

exactly like that we are passing through the world

but we think the world is passing us by

a cavalier of absence raised dust and galloped away

he's gone

only his dust remains

when searching for God and truth

look straight ahead

not to the right or to the left

his dust is always right here

but he has gone to the land of absence

I said:

o friend, are you truly my beloved?

I gaze at you and see that you are my soul

if you gave up on me

I would change my religion

you are my faith and my heresy both

o heart

even though you've been broken and disgraced

be honest

how can you not be deserving of love?

love is a fire

and you haven't even a drop of water

to put it out

come to your senses

you're just dreaming

ney* said:

my feet were stuck in mud for years

then one day a tyrant cut my neck out of whim

and opened nine wounds

you need to excuse me

if I cry out and wail with every breath

you can't get the taste of ecstasy

so long as you stay sober

you can't know the soul

so long as you think you are only your body

you will never reach the truth

if you don't give up your self

---

*a reed flute

God tells us:

o restless one

abandon people

you are ours, our true one

get used to us and acquire our habits

because the time will come when there will be

no time

and you will have to stand completely alone

I went to see my doctor:

"o doctor," I said

"tell me the truth

what cure is there for a person like me who has

fallen hopelessly in love?"

he thought for a moment

and then advised me:

"annihilate yourself

and give up everything that exists"

if you stay fooled by the empty promises of the flesh

you'll never know your essence

bring your mind back up into your head

the beloved is inside of you

senses are the essence of the body

but the essence of the senses is the soul

if you go beyond body, senses, and soul alike

everything becomes the beloved

it's not just your thoughts that are all bound up

your feet are tied up too

there's a secret to be found in action

movement turns boredom into joy

that's why the water from a fountain or river

tastes better than water sitting in a glass

since we started seeing others

we're no longer one

we've become multiple

when we started labeling things as good and bad

that's where the trouble started

the heart that hasn't learned ecstasy

will always stay under foot

the one who was gazing at me yesterday

has either the soul of an angel

or the spirit of a fairy

anyone who lives without seeing this beautiful face

might as well be dead

knowledge of anything without him

just stems from ignorance

yesterday the beloved was so kind as to ask me

"how can you live without me?"

"like a fish without water" I said

"but that's not possible," the beloved answered

and wept for me

even if the beloved skinned me alive

I still wouldn't yell or cry out

because that pain comes from him

he's our only friend

everyone else is our enemy

and friends don't complain about friends to enemies

I became crazy

really insane

and insane people never sleep

they don't even know where they might find

the path that leads to sleep

God too never sleeps

so God's insane people are simply taking after God

you have two hands, two feet, and two eyes

but it's a mistake to count the heart and the

beloved as two

even to say "the beloved"

isn't quite right

because God is the beloved

and whoever would call God a part of two

just doesn't have it right

I am a mountain

I hear the echo of the beloved

I am a painting

the beloved is my painter

do you really thing that all these words I've said

belong to me?

no, they're just the sound of the key turning in

the lock

if there's no fire in the heart

what is this smoke?

if aloe wood doesn't burn

what is this smell?

If I still exist

how can I die into love?

why does the moth yearn to be burned

in the flame of the candle?

fate rarely follows our heart's desire

existence is but a stepping stone

on the way to absence

our nanny watches us from behind a curtain

but all that we see is our shadows

we don't live here

⟳

if you look carefully

you will see that every particle

on the earth and in the sky

is as crazy and insane as we are

cheerful or somber they just keep on turning

lost in the sun of absence

the heart is a candle

waiting to be lit and illuminated

because of separation from the beloved

it feels ripped and torn

and needs to be sewn back together

if you don't know how to make the heart burn

listen to this:

love is something to encounter

not to learn

I'm a crazy, insane, and ruined man

hold my hand

because of you I'm utterly confused

and my head is spinning

hold my hand

every poor invalid is looked after by someone

I'm your poor and needy friend

hold my hand

this isn't spring

this is another season altogether

the spark in every eye

comes with its unique flavor of union

every branch is moving

but each one stirs for a different reason

moved by a different wind

o beauty

no one in this world is as pure and clean as you

no one is more elegant and charming

there will always be compromises and arguments

on the way of love

but as long as you're my friend

that's enough for me

the one who's peaceful and happy

isn't attached to wealth or poverty

less or more

he cares neither for the world

for people

nor even for himself

he's gone beyond

and has left no trace behind

dervishes should never be vain

conceit weighs as a heavy burden in their hearts

poverty and simplicity

are essential on the way to the beloved

pomp and splendor

are just thorns on that path

how long will you be concerned

about the needs of this soul?

how long will you worry

about this world full of trouble and fights?

the world can only take away your body and flesh

look upon your body as a garbage bag

and don't worry

when your lifeless body goes back to the ground

your soul will return to its place above the sky

if a violet can grow from black dirt

why wouldn't the cypress in this beautiful garden

grow fruit?

love has been so generous and kind

to offer us so much wine

so if you wake up with a hangover

blame yourself

not the drink

one who carries bricks to the mill

is dirty when he returns

you've already had enough of this drunkenness

but I'm not even close to having had enough yet

I feel annihilated at the very place where you

still exist

as long as water runs through its arches

the mill stones turn and wail silently

do you really expect to feel good

after you've done something bad?

badness just keeps on reaping badness

God is compassionate

and feels pity for everyone

but you can't harvest wheat if you sow barley

o heart

how do you expect to escape this confusion

and doubt?

listen to these words carefully:

if ever for a second you think you're not one

with God

at that moment you become a polytheist

because you've just attributed a partner to God

don't reveal secrets to those who don't believe

don't tell the beloved's story to an outcast

don't speak to strangers who can't understand

don't talk to a thorn-eating camel about

anything but thorns

❧

o one who is so alive with the soul of this world

shame on you!

why are you being like that?

don't avoid love out of fear that you may die

die into love so that you may stay alive

when your heart is cleansed of everything you

think you are

you'll see yourself as an old beloved soul

it's not possible to see your face without a mirror

so gaze at the beloved

let his face become your mirror

you don't think the road you're on is the road to union

you don't think you can find soul in this world

the fountain from which Hizur* drank the waters of life

is right on your way

but you filled the fountain with dirt

and dried up its waters

---

*Hizur is a legendary being who is reputed to arrive and help in critical moments; he drank the water of life and became immortal.

the essence of insanity is love

the soul has gone and gotten lost

and the mind has turned itself upside down

hundreds of deserts are burning

with the fires of our love

❦

one soul feeds on thoughts and sorrows

but another is like a lion moving freely in the forest

thought is like a chisel

put your mind in your head

and don't think about a thing

be careful though

don't stub your toe

you say your saints live inside the circle of being

and becoming

but the dot of your heart is bigger

than the throne in the center of this circle

when your heart eats the troubles inside you like fodder

you escape this world and reach union

you are the light of my heart

you give peace and comfort to my soul

you also create troubles some time

you ask me

where are the signs and the evidence of the beloved?

the lack of any sign or evidence whatsoever

is the sign and evidence of this beloved

I decided to follow the drunks and became

drunk along with them

I got lost in their ecstasy

and became disgusted with my mind

in order to be admitted into the asylum of love

I went completely crazy and lost my mind

you're not a slave

so start talking like a sultan

throw the arrow of your gaze wherever you like

since you are free of both yourself and others

beat the drum of God endlessly

∽✧∾

your soul has been purified by growing old

your body has been cleansed by wearing out

you're in a fire, burning

this fire is your heaven

this fire is your eternal garden

if I could hear your voice

my voice would become beautiful too

I would become endless like God's grace

you've bought me a hundred times

I'm yours

even so, buy me once more

so I can give birth to myself again

o soul

I've lost my soul as well as the universe

o moon

I've lost the earth as well as the sky

don't hand me to my hand

pour me right me into my mouth

through your drunkenness I've lost the way to

my mouth

I'll just walk around drunk today

I'll turn my skull into a cup for wine today

I'll run around the city shit-faced

be on the lookout for a wise man

let's help him go completely crazy and insane today

❦

I'm so sweet and beautiful all by myself

who needs sugarcane?

my warmth doesn't come from fire or water

love came and emptied me so much

that when I measure myself on a scale

I'm two stones lighter than absence

thoughts and signs come from the mind

but the beloved comes only from love

thoughts are like sullied water

but love is the pure water of life

you can ascend to the sky by following signs

but you won't find any trace of lovers there

I dissolved like salt in the clear sea of purity

neither doubt nor blasphemy remained

a star arose in my heart

it exploded and disappeared into the seven skies

❧

you got me drunk in the house of prayer

you led me to Mecca but made me pray to idols

I don't understand your virtues or your games

but go ahead and use me however you want

I am in your hand

o source of joy and pleasure

stay close by

don't leave us

you were once the grape of absence

but then they turned you into wine

o wine, don't go back to being a grape

don't be shy

come on in

join us

the body without discipline

simply eats or sleeps

the sound of the rebab

is coming from the sema*

gathering

enter their circle

start doing sema

---

*Sema is the spiritual practice of the Sufis. While different Sufi schools will focus on different practices, sema might include whirling and spontaneous movements, breathing exercises, and chants.

be a falcon in your rapture

be a lion in your majesty

find the treasure of the contented soul

walk fast

get to the place where neither fast nor slow exist

ascend to the height where there is no high or low

it doesn't matter whether I wear spring or fall colors

I'm still just me

in fact, if one of them didn't exist

neither the rose bloom nor its thorns could grow

differences in appearances are only in the eyes

the rose garden laughs at those kinds of eyes

when love for the beloved first seized me

I would cry out so loud at night

that my neighbors couldn't sleep

now my wailing has diminished

but my love has grown even stronger

smoke disappears

when the flame burns brightly

what use is there for advice
now that I've fallen into your love?
"tie his feet down" they say about me
but it's my heart that's gone crazy
what's the use of tying my feet?

❧

if you close your eyes to earthly concerns
your heart will turn into an eye
and you will look out onto different worlds
as long as you don't become cocky
everything you do will be admired

do good deeds

time recognizes the merit

and never forgets the goodness

of good deeds

everyone is going to die some day

and their belongings will remain in this world

the goodness that you made

while in this world

will be the inheritance that you take to the next

if you fall in love

still stay calm

be as sharp as a thorn

so that the beloved

like a rose

can press you to his heart

and take you to his side

when the dawn of God's love breaks

the souls of all God's creatures

open their wings

and start to fly

humans reach such a place

that they can see the beloved

without opening their eyes

I want a beloved

who causes nothing but trouble

he should have fire in his heart

and shed blood at will

he screams to the sky

and fights with the stars

plunging into oceans

couldn't put out his fire

this solitude is better

than being together with thousands

this freedom is sweeter

than owning the whole world

this talking with God

even if only for a very short moment

is better than anything

look at your eyes carefully

they see inside as well as out

if you observe those insane with love

you will see

that someone

is looking out through their eyes

who is it?

don't go anywhere

but to the gatherings of lovers and drunks

don't get involved with normal people

everyone pulls you to their side

the raven to ruin

the parrot to sweetness

lovers would give up both worlds
and sacrifice hundreds of years of life
for just one moment together
they jump through thousands of hoops
after the smell of one breath
and would sacrifice thousands of lives
to satisfy a single heart

if alligators infested the seas
and tigers took over the plains
lovers would still keep their eyes fixed
on the beautiful face of their friend

❧

if you start on the journey
the road will be opened for you
if you die to yourself
you'll be carried all the way to God
if you've been so humiliated
that you can't fit into this world
your light will still shine through
even though you're not there

there's no room in the tavern

for cockiness and conceit

only brave and decent people

can enter here

once you're in, go ahead and gamble

maybe you'll win

maybe you'll lose

maybe you'll end up checkmated

o love

who are you?

you are everything

everything is you

joy and sorrow come from you

you leave people shaken and confused

o love

all gold comes from your mind

you are the mother

all of humanity are your children

every particle of the body

is hungry for the food

at God's table

they rush to eat and drink there

but then stay for all eternity

they can't tear themselves away

from this divine meal

every sensation

every image

every thing we think lifeless

talks to us silently

without lips or tongue

relating to us our joys and sorrows

informing us

trying to awaken us

"why are you so cold to your brother?" they say

how sad to be unaware of the messages

coming from the unformed ones

even the denial of God

comes from God

but no one knows that

"is there sugar on your ruby red lips?" I asked

he said "no"

but this denial

is also a kind of sugar

I come from the soul of souls

I come from the place of placelessness

the way to that place has no end

you can walk there

but you can't use your head or feet

let the beloved be your head

let the beloved be your feet

there's a road from the soul to my heart

and the heart

tirelessly

searches for that road

when the heart becomes as pure and clear as water

the moon can be seen

as a reflection in the heart

you come here this morning drunk and confused
I can tell that last night's wine
has left you like this
today is the day to nurse your hangover
not the day to run around doing business
it's better that you stay home today
as a leftover from last night

don't ever think that the dervish

who humiliates himself before people

and dies to himself before God

is feeding on an illusion

the imperial tent of that beautiful soul

is pitched beyond existence

far beyond the universe

the water of life

is concealed as a divine gift

inside this body

and that's why you can't see it

the self has gone and placed

a seal on the heart

and hid love away forever

break the seal

save the love

why are you so afraid?

there are secret paths in the heart

go and find the beloved

you think I've taken the wrong path

by becoming a drunk

while you, o hodja*

have remained a sober and wise man

you boast about your piety and prayers

but you should know very well

that such boasting

doesn't even take you so far

as the foot of the bridge

---

*a learned man

there isn't a sign

marking the valley of love

but you'll find

throngs of people there

desperate with hope

o heart, never give up your hope

willow trees can grow dates

in the soul's garden

I died to myself

every particle of my body exploded into the sky

so ecstatic

so drunk

yet I still stay in this dungeon

with all its faults and foolishness

I'm so happy

because all your sorrows

fit inside my heart

there all your troubles can be put to rest

and dissolved in the light

your grief is so big

that the earth and sky can't contain it

and yet it can fit

in a space in my heart

that's no bigger than the eye of a needle

love has no beginning

love has no end

love never dies

love lives eternal

so many people search for love

on the day of resurrection

but everyone except the lovers

will be dragged out from the temple

if fortune smiles constantly on your face

don't let it go to your head

getting drunk on a glass of sherbert

would just embarrass your lover

❦

greed is the source of all your problems

if you become too fond of women and food

you'll never get out of your troubles

just like a bird who falls for the bait

gets caught in the trap

and lives in a small cage hanging from the ceiling

if you know the true nature

of existence and absence both

then neither can be a problem for you

leaving the world of appearances behind

you become the truth

distinctions of any kind no longer matter

how could anyone

who plays with you

ever be sad?

how could anyone

whom your light turns into the sun

ever be gloomy?

how could the secrets of the world stay secret

from anyone who becomes your best friend?

joy doesn't come because of sorrow

yet nothing but the pangs I feel for you in my heart

could ever cure me of my troubles

I was thinking to say this and that when we met

but when I finally saw you

I couldn't even breathe

I travel hundreds of miles beyond reason

I go past good and bad deeds both

there are so many breathtaking beauties

to be found beyond this veil

o foolish ones

if you want to find me

fall in love with who you are

night has gone

where did it go?

it went back to where it came from

so that we too could go back home

o night, when you return again from that

promised land

talk to us

tell us how we can turn our suffering into love

no disease remains for the one who drinks

the waters of life from the beloved's cup

no thorn remains in the rose

picked from the beloved's garden

they say there's a window between hearts

but there aren't even any walls left

never mind the windows

you said the beloved was the moon

but you made a mistake

what's the moon?

then you said the sultan

but that's wrong too

who's the sultan?

"we're getting up too early"

how long will you be telling me that?!

I'm with the sun now

how can you call this early?

love struck me like lightning

and left its smell behind

I gave away all my belongings

I've only this patched cloak left

the creek of love

that I barely had to raise my skirt to pass through

turned into a torrent

and rose up to my neck

the person who knows even a bit of the secret

will fall in love

lose his mind

and find his way back home

the person who's truly crazy and insane

is the one

who after seeing your face

doesn't go crazy and start acting insane

the sleeping head over there on the pillow

is missing out on his company

if you feel him in your heart

how could you ever sleep?!

gazing into my eyes all night long

love tells me:

"take pity on whoever sleeps without this"

gifts of kindness come to the one

who suffers from loving the beloved

the beloved tells him:

"during your short life on earth

search for union

union is the only answer

to the silent scream of your short life"

death can never harm you

because you can never lose your soul

you came to this earth from the sky

again you will return to the sky

a spark from your fire

fell into me

waters of joy flowed from your words

into the river of my heart

but now I understand:

that water was a mirage

that spark was like lightning

struck and gone

everything has been a dream

only memory remains

that great, heart catching beauty

is closer to us than our soul

I never even call out to him

because the only one you have to call out to

is the one who isn't here

my beloved takes me away to such a beautiful place

he carries off my body

and takes my soul as well

I give him all kinds of excuses not to go

but he just tells me:

"if you don't come willingly

I'll drag you there by force"

the heart that doesn't carry your secret love in it

can't be Muslim

must belong to an infidel

the city that you don't rule over

even if prosperous

must be seen as a ruin

soul turned its face to me and said:

give up your how's and what's

and just gaze into infinity

the meaning of creation and the secret of love

have been concealed up until now

but they're starting to come out

from behind the curtains

the master cut a piece of cane from the reed bed

he opened nine holes and called it Adam*

o ney, you wail when my lips touch you

but you should see instead

that my lips are giving you

the breath of life

❦

whoever tries to see you

with just the eyes of the head

looks like a fool staring at a wise man

don't try to awaken with sleep still in your eyes

because that seeing can't see the secret things

---

*Humans have nine openings in their body.

lovers are such strange people

they're not like everybody else

they don't carry their souls in their bodies

instead, their souls carry them

people run to the the river of the waters of life

in hopes of becoming immortal

yet the waters of life

are always running to the lovers

when your love starts wrestling with my heart

your soul gets scared

and runs barefoot out the back door

I'm a lover

you're crazy if you think I'm wise

if you're wise and want to stay that way

you'll stay away from me

we found our cure in love
we bled for love every moment
love is our friend every moment
every moment love breathes us

love is a calamity
nothing but trouble
if you're scared of trouble
you can't be a lover
in love's business you have to be brave
when the fire of love
falls onto your soul
you have to surrender to the flame

such a love

that when it came

it blackened the rest

of what I thought love to be

I was burned

became ash

my ashes were scattered and disappeared

but when they found your scent

my ashes came back

and formed into thousands of shapes again

wherever divine grace can be felt to exist

distinctions between things drop completely away

rosaries and organs no longer serve any purpose

a believer from Rum and a tribesman from Africa

are one and the same

everyone has to surrender to this

or keep hitting his head against a stone wall forever

they say there's a beautiful paradise to come

where pure and clean wine

will be served by kole eyed houries*

since the end is going to be like that

we decided not to wait

we grabbed our wine glasses

and are already sitting next to the beloved

---

*beautiful celestial black-eyed damsels of the Muslim paradise

there are other souls besides the one you carry

there are other loaves of bread besides the one you eat

there are other beauties besides the one you found

only the beloved is irreplaceable in this world

❧

hear the drunk shouting out to the sky

see the radiance of real beings

playing in the crucible of emptiness

withdraw from both worlds

and watch the great play

of those who've died to themselves

and been transported to absence

o my soul

the garden knows springtime

the cypress tree knows fall

but we never go anywhere

we just stay here

lift your veil and lock the door

yes, you and I are alone

the house is empty

o my soul

don't hang around with friends who are sad all the time

spend time with cheerful people of good heart

when you enter the garden

don't go directly to the thorns

stay next to the roses and jasmine instead

if you are longing for an unseen beloved

first go and find the lovers

get in their circle

stay there for a while

then leave the circle

go away from people

go directly to the creator

and stay there

you are a power

that governs over everything

you are a religion

in which it is impossible to break one's oath

you are a knowledge

that knows no boundaries

you are such a magician

that no one can get out of your trap

be a falcon in your effort

be a tiger in your strength

be an expert in hunting

be brave in war

don't hang around with the peacock and

the nightingale

one's conceited

the other talks too much

of all the troubles for you to choose

choose the trouble of love

I don't know of a better way to reach the beloved

don't worry if you don't have wealth and possessions

worry if you don't have the troubles of love

throw stones in the jar

of those who are ignorant

grab after the skirt of the wise

don't waste a single moment

with anyone who's incompetent

a mirror will be rusted

if you throw it into water

bairam* has come

the sultan gets all dressed up

but who in either world has ever seen

such a bairam as I have seen?

o heart

o soul

the world's treasure

was found in a secret place

this is the real bairam

in fact, it's thousands of bairams

---

*a Muslim festival celebrated at the close of the fast of Ramadan and, again, seventy days after the fast

night says:
I'm a friend to the wine drinkers
I give comfort to the brokenhearted
but I'm the angel of death
at the doors of the ones
who'll have nothing to do with love

❦

love is an ocean
that has no bottom
has no coast
an ocean that is suspended
submerge yourself in this ocean
and live there forever
one drop from this sea gives you hope
anything else gives you nothing but fear

time came to embrace you

and turn your soul

into a house of fire

there's a gold mine

hidden deep inside your soul

I burn you

to purify you

I'm happy

because I'm saved

from the happinesses of this world

I'm happy

because I'm drunk without wine

I don't care what anybody else might think

my secret happiness

is all that I need

cupbearer, let me be your drunk this evening

I've waited for you all day long

serve me wine

and save me from the traps of both worlds

I'm yours tonight

all night long

there's no one like him

in either world

he's neither secretive nor open

neither up nor down

he has no peer

every arrow is thrown

from his taut bow

every subtle word

that has ever been spoken

comes from his mouth

the whole universe stands in awe

before a single one of my particles

it's constantly looking for ways to help me

the sun and sky are the slave and servant

of my turning star

both worlds got lost

when they went looking for me

he's hidden in the garden

over there

under the trees

he takes so many different forms

but he is what he is

an endless ocean that covers over everything

from a single wave of his ocean

hundreds of waves of soul are born

when I see you smile

I have to smile too

I'm just crazy

for your mouthless, lipless grin

it's too bad

no one sees your smile as I do

but most people don't have the eyes to see it

tell the musician

who still needs sheets of music

who can't yet read

from the book of the heart

tell him:

if poems and melodies hide their faces from you

look at my face

and read them there

what can I do?

an amazing beauty just came to me

and I'm left feeling drunk in my head

what can I do?

I used to be so devout on this path

but what can I do

now that this beauty has given me a kiss?

forgive me

if I get cocky and conceited at times

I'm just your drunk

don't rush me to my death

you already have me in your hand

you tell me:

"I've created such a big world

for you to play in"

but you tied down my feet

so where could I go?

don't try to repent

every time I try

my vow just gets broken

my drunk soul

doesn't want to repent again

I vowed a hundred times

a thousand times

not to do this or that

repentance just got tired of me

put your mind back in your head, o heart

that's where the beloved is

he's listening from behind the curtain

we're like the ney

our wailings and cryings don't come from us

all this moaning, groaning, and heavy breathing

come from him

look at your body as a whole

it looks like a sprawl of drunks

who've fallen asleep on top of each other

if you want them to be your friends

then wake each of them up

don't just step on them and go on your way

❦

if you've got a brain in your head

and can see things clearly

then hold your tongue

and save yourself

once the fish quit talking

no one could separate its head from its body

crazy winter came

and with it long nights

we too look like a pitch-dark night

our love goes on forever

all desire for sleep disappeared from our heart

but whoever needs to sleep

should at least stretch his legs first

the beloved snuck up behind me

and touched my hand today

suddenly I lost myself

and my body exploded

I'm not one

but a thousand times drunk today

I've gone totally crazy and insane

today I can only worship

those who've gone crazy and insane

the wind of your love

has been blowing in my head

all day long

I've felt restless and drunk on your love all day

usually drunkenness leaves after a few hours

but I've stayed drunk

all day long

my love is purer than clean, clear water

I'll play any love game you want

ordinary love is so fickle

it changes from moment to moment

but the love for my beloved

goes on forever

o beloved

my heart is overflowing with words

but my tongue is all tied up

and I can't say a thing

it doesn't get more bizarre than this:

I'm so thirsty

and pure, clean water is flowing right in front of me

but I can't open my mouth to drink

the first time I saw love

I threw my heart and soul under its feet

then I asked myself:

can the lover and the beloved really be two?

they're only one

I must have been cross-eyed

I can't even speak

about this blinding, suffocating world

so submerged in sorrow

but I don't really care anymore

music gives me so much joy

you can take my pawn but not my king

I disappeared while gazing at the king

who cares about one less pawn?

I won't grant you your wish

if you don't give me your heart

if you don't do what I ask

I won't give you what you want

quit being so false

and don't play dead

I swear on your soul and your heart

I won't give myself to you

until you melt away completely

come to your senses

dawn separates night from day

time to drink morning wine

time to light another candle besides the sun and

the moon

then take a spark from that fire

throw it on the tent of the mind

and burn it to the ground

you'll never be safe in a crowd of people

if you're nosy and make too much noise

you'll never free yourself from all of your troubles

by talking too much in all the wrong places

try hard

stay silent

so you can stay away from all the problems

of "I" and "you"

what am I to do

if the cupbearer offers red wine?

what am I to do

if the beloved

brighter than the moon

gives me a kiss?

if I'm seized by the joy of union today

I'd be stupid to start talking about tomorrow

I can't explain the secrets
even to those who can hear them
they're inside me like gut feelings
but I just can't put my finger on "this is it"

❦

your love makes knowledge look like a blunder
what's love?
what's knowledge?
what and whom can we know?
in fact there is only one we should know
both worlds depend on him
both worlds cry out for him
he is the only one who exists
yet we don't know who he is

there's a wine that spreads the wings of soul's bird
that never makes you tired or boring
love is the cupbearer of that wine
lovers drink gladly from the cupbearer's hand
that wine's not forbidden to us

ᔥᔥ

I just came from there
my sins, apologies, and guilts all got burnt
I've brought back a fire you've never seen before
it says: "step aside
I burn down everything but God"

every day

this beauty of love

finds a new way to look beautiful

every day

he hangs a different book

of love around his neck

God put thorns around love's door

to stop anyone who's not a lover from entering

a man of love told me today:

if you're a rind*

hang out with other rinds

yesterday's gone

and has become nothing

never mind about nothing

tomorrow's not here

so don't even talk about it

---

*an unconventional, free-living person who lives by his own rules

I became spellbound by your eyes

your love lit and brightened

the candle of my soul

I fixed my eyes on your face

may God save us from eyes that aren't like this

❧

the more attention I pay

to the things that I do

I realize my vision's no good

but why should I even bother with my two eyes?

let me watch the world through yours

thank God I've reached you again
I'm free from the ropes of separation
this time I drank so much of the wine of absence
that I'm going to stay drunk forever

❦

I hope this hunched back sky
will store all the words we spoke
while we were sitting here alone
then one day
it will pour rain on this world
and our secrets will grow like grass

God made us spend

the entire night

from dusk 'til dawn

with wine and pleasure

he made us celebrate bairam

even though we hadn't finished Ramadan

you're the one

the best of people

please fill our glass

serve us

get us drunk

then send our greetings out

to the corners of the world

I thought if I put the leash of repentance

on the neck of self's dog

I could control and wear him out

but whenever he sees a carcass in the road

he breaks the chain and attacks

what am I going to do with this dog?

❧

love is a glass

I'm the most happy drunk

love is a wedding party

I'm the drummer

I love the love

that doesn't let a man do his job

because I become idle

when I get too busy with earthly things

our cloak is made from his cloth
our heart is like dice in his hand
our path is his drunken eyes
our religion is to love him

I'm so tired of this material world
with all its temporary things
it's time to see the real beauty
but when I gaze at him
I see myself
and when I look at myself
I see him

we keep turning like the sky

in love with the moon

only God knows our situation

we can't figure out how smart people

can keep their minds in their heads

when they see what's really going on in the world

oh well, they can't figure us out either

we aren't the village headman

we are kalanderi*

we don't live at the palace

we're ordinary people

no, no

we're like a pen in the hand of a painter

we don't know where we are

we don't know who we are

---

*a particularly unconventional Sufi sect whose only interest was in having direct experience of God

the wine that's forbidden to ordinary people

is served again and again

to the one who's freed himself from all boundaries

keep offering us more

don't tell us: "no wine is left"

where do we begin?

where do we end?

I removed the crown of selfishness from the

top of my head

I threw it away

and it struck a stone

I now wear the belt of service

that honors you

separation was laughing

while I was crying before

but now I'm the one who's laughing

while separation cries

when sorrow departs

and finally leaves you alone

it removes your human gown

and turns you into a sage

you become a strange sort of soul

who doesn't care about a thing

and no one cares about you

how could you hope to become his friend

if you don't understand that?

work hard with your pain

I can cure you

don't gaze at anyone but me

I'm the only one you need to know

don't say I'm dead

be grateful

I'm the price you need to pay for your life

how can we refuse his kind offer?
we're but the work of the artist
so let's go to where the artist lives
golden bowls are set for us in the sky
why should we be satisfied
with water on the table?

❧

let's take a walk in the moonlight
let's go into the rose garden
and watch the sleepless daffodils
for three months our ship skidded around on the ice
the time has come, o brother
let's sail away together on the water

how long will I turn into dust and dirt

chasing after worthless things?

I'll climb the mountain instead

and hide inside a cave

how long will I rest

like a sleeping baby

in the arms of beauty?

now is the time for turning and spinning

turning around the creator

when I feel a twinge of desire
it's always you that I want
I set the table last night with your love
then I had a dream
but I can't remember what it was
all I know is that I woke up this morning
completely drunk

love is my only friend

love was with me before I came into this world

and is with me still

soul is the lazy one on the path of love

love yells and screams:

"come on

hurry up

reach me"

I'm only a particle

you are my sun

I'm sick with grief

you are my cure

I keep flying behind you

without arms or wings

I'm like a piece of straw

you are my magnet

how can the sun match the beauty of your face?

the fastest wind can't touch a single thread of your hair

even reason

who is king at the city of existence

goes completely crazy

when he reaches your town

I don't know what it is inside of me

that makes me smile all the time

only God knows that

but my heart is like a branch of a rose tree

swaying constantly in the morning breeze

❧

if hell is the only place where I can touch your hair

I feel sorry for the ones who've gone to heaven

if they call me to the steps of paradise without you

I'd rather stay on an endless plain

at the break of dawn

an early morning breeze passes by scattering musk

friend, where does that beautiful smell come from?

wake up

why are you sleeping?

life is passing us by

don't miss that beautiful smell

a caravan of musk is passing right now

forgive this sleepless servant

forgive the thirsty people who don't have water

forgive

because the one who doesn't know how to forgive

can't get close to God

❦

without love

there can be no joy or happiness

no beauty

no harmony in the world

even if hundreds of raindrops fall from the cloud

no secret pearls can be found in the sea

without the rhythms of love

my beauty had his feelings hurt

by my constantly reciting verses

he told me:

"are you measuring me with the meters of the poem?"

I said:

"tell me what verse you'd like me to recite"

he answered:

"how could I fit into any one verse?"

I exist

but this glass of morning wine also exists

I think

I get up

I walk around

I get drunk in front of the tall cypress

then melt completely away

so that nothing remains but him

he clapped his hands when he saw me drunk

"he's broken his vow again

and is staggering around like a drunk"

repentance is like a glass blower

it's hard to make a bottle

easy to break it

many struggles take place at the table of union

which has been set since the beginning of time

so much has been eaten at that table

and yet the table remains unchanged

nothing is missing

just like a bird that lands on top of a mountain

and then flies away

look and see

nothing is added to or taken off the mountain

sit next to God's lovers

so that the smoke of your sorrow can be dispersed

and your confusions cleared away

don't think about their faults

because they know your thoughts

even before you think them

Translator's Afterword

*I*f death didn't come to humans, we would be reasonably happy following the voice of reason as the most trustworthy guide in our lives. But death comes, sooner or later, without exception, making everything else obsolete.

The silence after an obituary defies all consolations of faith and makes any explanations based on reason futile. Reincarnation, hell, and heaven are our bad habits of applying the theory of cause and effect to both the origin of life and to that which lies beyond our life. Even reason knows that we have no right to think this way. We would only know about life if we could die and come back again: "A fish will know water if it could know air," says Mevlana (the name Rumi is more commonly known by in the lands where he lived his life).

"You ride your horse to the edge of the water," Mevlana says.

"You need something lighter to go beyond." Reason cannot comprehend nothingness. Annihilation of self, for Mevlana, is the only way toward *itlak,* or absolute liberation. The rest is all fiction and literature.

> *"You'll never get my fragrance unless you die first."*
> MEVLANA

> *"Death is going to beat everyone, why not beat Death*
> *before your death?"*
> SHUSHUD (A MODERN SUFI TEACHER)

Mevlana brings immortality to our backyard.

I would like to extend my gratitude to Will Johnson and Asuman Tezcan for their careful attentiveness to my work and for their very kind help. The rubais presented here are not only beautiful, they also have the smell of absence, served from Will's glass. They come from 1,765 rubais written in the second volume of Rumi's *Divan-i Kebir.** They are for the lovers, not the scholars. Yet even so, I am often questioned by people from both the scholastic and the more orthodox

---

*Limited editions of the replica of this two-volume *Divan,* handwritten in 1368, have been available since January 2007 through the Society for Understanding Mevlana (28 South Norfolk Street, San Mateo, California, 94401, nevite@msn .com, www.sfumevlana.org). The *Divan* replica with English translations (a four-volume set) will follow.

Islamic communities who find it difficult to believe that Rumi could have actually said these things.

The English translations that appear in this volume have been cross-referenced from several sources. The fourteenth-century compilers of the original *Divan* placed all the rubais into the second volume (where they can be found on pages 256–89, 313–14, 322–40, and 342–44). We have also based our work on translations by Abdulbaki Golpinarli, Professor Bediuzzaman Furuzanfer, and Sefic Can. Anyone wishing to verify the sources on which our translations are based may do so through contacting the Society for Understanding Mevlana, care of the contact information in the preceding note.

NEVIT O. ERGIN, M.D.
SAN MATEO, CALIFORNIA
SEPTEMBER 2006

Books of Related Interest

The Forbidden Rumi
The Suppressed Poems of Rumi on Love, Heresy, and Intoxication
Translations and commentary by Nevit O. Ergin and Will Johnson

The Spiritual Practices of Rumi
Radical Techniques for Beholding the Divine
by Will Johnson

Yoga of the Mahamudra
The Mystical Way of Balance

Commentary by Abd al-Kerım al-Jıli
Translated from the Arabic by Rabia Terry Harris

The Way of Sufi Chivalry
by Ibn al-Husayn al-Sulami
An interpretation by Tosun Bayrak al-Jerrahi

The Book of Sufi Healing
by Shaykh Hakim Moinuddin Chishti

Muhammad
His Life Based on the Earliest Sources
by Martin Lings

Inner Traditions • Bear & Company
P.O. Box 388 • Rochester, VT 05767
1-800-246-8648
www.InnerTraditions.com

Or contact your local bookseller